The Weight of the Wait

A 30 Day Devotional for Single Women

Tavara Johnson

The Weight of the Wait: A 30 Day Devotional for Single Women

Copyright © 2018 by Tavara Johnson

Published in the United States of America by
ChosenButterflyPublishing LLC

ChosenButterfly Publishing

www.cb-publishing.com
Editing by Stephanie Montgomery, Unique Communications
Concepts

All Scriptures taken from the KING JAMES VERSION (KJV): KING
JAMES Public Domain

ISBN: 978-1-945377-05-1
First Edition Printing
Printed in the United States of America
March 2018

This book is dedicated to all singles who are fighting the good fight of faith and enduring the 'weight of the wait'. Trust the plans God has for you and know that as long as marriage is in His will for your life, you will meet your God-ordained mate.

Foreword

Singleness is not a concluded condition but a temporary state of preparation. With this in mind, I am humbled and profoundly proud of Tavara Johnson. One who has stood the test of time as a Single Woman who loves the Lord. This devotional will provoke one to stand firm in God recognizing that our completeness is in Him. For it's in God, we live, move and have our being. As a single woman you have greater liberties to serve the Lord and allow Him to mold and shape you into a refined vessel that's equipped for every good work. As you read the volume of this Powerful devotional, may the Power of Elohim transform your life, make you whole and equip you for a Glorious future in God.

Kingdom Blessings,
Associate Pastor Clarice Thompson
Global Outreach Ministries.

Introduction

We are living in an instant, 'microwave society' and an 'I want what I want by any means necessary' world today. The reality is that depending on what we are waiting for - the wait may be easier in one area than another. For singles waiting on a spouse, the wait might be more daunting than waiting for a new job. I have come to realize that during your time of singleness is when you should prepare for the next level, based on what God has promised you. In my opinion, singles are looked-down upon in society and once women begin approaching the age of thirty - panic tends to set in. Those waiting in expectation for marriage must realize that being married will not solve problems of loneliness if that is an issue of concern. Marriage will only solve the problem of celibacy for singles that are struggling with their flesh.

This devotional is for single women who are in their waiting season. This book will reassure the single woman that she is not alone and that others all over the world are experiencing a similar journey. It is my desire that singles will be encouraged, inspired and empowered as they reflect on each day.

Tavara Johnson

Day 1

Know Your Worth

Scripture Reading: *"Give not that which is holy unto the dogs, neither cast ye your pearls before swine, lest they trample them under their feet, and turn again and rend you."* Matthew 7:6

One of the first steps to identifying your worth is to know what the word of God says about you. It is important to understand that dogs and pigs cannot comprehend the significance of pearls, which are unique gemstones. Because of this, you may meet someone who has a swine or dog mind-set without the capacity to have an appreciation for the person you are and what you have to offer. Always ask the Holy Spirit to give you the discernment to know when someone is unable to identify your value and worth. Since God is our Father, He works diligently to protect us from these types of individuals.

However, we must be mindful to work along with Him and not against Him. Perhaps this can mean severing ties with people when He asks you. Can you recall a friendship or relationship where no matter what you did to show appreciation to that person - they were simply unable to realize how valuable you were to them? How did it make you feel? Were you misused because of their inability to see how precious you were? Whenever you find yourself having to sell who you are as an individual to others, this is an indication that the relationship or friendship is not for you.

Day 1 - Know your Worth Reflections

1. How can you tell when you have lowered your worth or standards? And how did this make you feel?

_____

_____

_____

2.What steps should you take to regain your worth?

_____

_____

_____

_____

3. How do you handle situations where others have made you feel less than because of your standards?

_____

_____

_____

_____

4. How often do you pray for God to increase your discernment in hopes of reducing the amount of persons who cannot appreciate your value from entering your life?

_____

_____

_____

_____

_____

Know your Worth Prayer

Father, help me to believe what your word says about how valuable I am to you so that I may understand that you only desire the best for me. Connect me with individuals who will celebrate me and not tolerate me. Provide me with the discernment to know from afar, whom I should allow into my life and personal space. Amen.

Day 2

Putting God First

Scripture Reading: *"But seek ye first the kingdom of God, and His righteousness; and all these things shall be added unto you"* Matthew 6:33

If you desire to know God and wish to discover His righteousness, you will have to seek Him. Seeking involves actively looking for something. The desires and goals of many - along with the hustle and bustle of everyday life causes us to place God on the back burner. In most cases, He usually receives the time we have left over after everything on our agenda is completed. How do you think this makes Him feel? God wants to know that He is first in our lives above all other things. The Bible admonishes that our focus should not be pursuing material things - but rather God. The various ways you can seek Him are through the word of God and prayer to name a few. While seeking God's kingdom, all other things - such as spiritual and physical blessings, will manifest as He longs to see His children successful. The book of John states that He came that we might have life and have it more abundantly. We can find hope in the assurance God gave us and trust that His word will not return unto Him void.

1.What are some of the ways you can re-organize your time/schedule to ensure you put God first?

_____

_____

_____

_____

_____

2. Do you think your level of intimacy with God affects how you prioritize with Him?

_____

_____

_____

_____

3. Are you more fascinated with the blessings of God than the person Himself?

_____

_____

_____

_____

4. How often do you pursue God as your last resort after failing in your own strength? How do you think this makes God feel?

_____

_____

_____

_____

_____

Putting God First Prayer

Lord, help me to place you first above everything in this world. Provide me with strategies that will assist me in balancing my everyday life and prevent me from giving you the leftovers of my time. I desire a deeper level of intimacy with you and want to learn more about you. Amen

Day 3

Trust God's Plans

Scripture Reading: *"For I know the thoughts that I think toward you, saith the LORD, thoughts of peace, and not of evil, to give you an expected end."*
Jeremiah 29:11

God has the blue print for your life and you must have confidence that He is aware of exactly where you are in life. As you spend intimate time with God, He will reveal His purpose for your life. You might ask; how can I be sure that I am truly hearing from God? The book of John chapter 10 states that the enemy's desire is to steal, kill and destroy - so this means that he will not lead you to a life of advancement, but rather you will endure a life of misery. On the other hand, if you are a child of the king, God says that you will know His voice.

However, God will always send confirmation and although He may ask for things, which might seem impossible - He will grant you the grace to achieve success. Most of all, despite your hesitations - there will be peace in your spirit. In some instances, you may feel inadequate or unworthy - but this is a normal feeling. Nevertheless, do not allow fear to prevent you from moving forward and living the abundant life that God has predestined for you.

Day 3 - Trust God's Plan Reflections

1. How much do you really trust God?

_____

_____

_____

_____

_____

2. Is it easier for you to trust Him with one area of your life than another? If yes, then why?

_____

_____

_____

_____

3. Do you feel the level of control you desire over your life makes it difficult for you to trust God? If yes, then what steps are you willing to take to give God your all?

_____

_____

_____

_____

_____

4. Are you aware of some of the plans God has for you?

_____

_____

_____

_____

_____

_____

Trust God's Plan Prayer

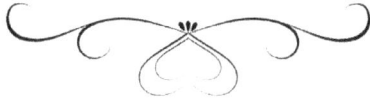

Father, help me to recognize the plans that you have for me. Send people who can assist me in accomplishing your will for my life. Give me the boldness to do what you have asked me to do despite my insecurities and the opinions of others. Amen

Day 4

The Weight of the Wait

Scripture Reading: *"But they that wait upon the LORD shall renew their strength; they shall mount up with wings as eagles; they shall run, and not be weary; and they shall walk, and not faint"*. Isaiah 40:31

We live in a 'microwave world' and society, which tells us we can have whatever we desire, whenever we want. However, waiting on God to bring your goals, visons and dreams to fruition is never easy. This is because most people have their whole life planned and the timing of every event in their life which they desire to take place. Over time, many become frustrated when they have fasted, prayed, decreed, and declared a thing to be established – however, it has yet to manifest.

The question individuals need to consider is whether what they desire is in the will of God. Recognize that God is aware of your exact location and He has the power to get you where needed. Truly waiting on God means to fully surrender your plans and will. The quicker we surrender our will to God with the expectation that He will work everything out in His timing - the sooner we will release unnecessary anxiety and begin to see manifestation in our lives. This will occur because we are no longer trying to accomplish our plans in our strength but are relying solely on the strength of God to complete the work He began in us.

Day 4 - The Weight of the Wait
Reflections

1. What are some of the consequences you endured from going ahead of God's timing?

_____

_____

_____

_____

_____

_____

_____

_____

2. Are you still currently dealing with those consequences to date? How detrimental were the consequences and were others affected by your decision?

_____

_____

_____

_____

_____

_____

_____

_____

3. Were you ever in a situation where your timing did not agree with God's timing? If yes, how did you handle the situation and how is your relationship with God now? Should you be embarrassed of your behaviour as a Christian?

_____

_____

_____

_____

_____

4. Have you fully surrendered you will to God as yet? Why or why not?

_____

_____

_____

_____

_____

_____

_____

The Weight of the Wait Prayer

Father, teach me how to truly wait on you and not go ahead of your timing. Give me the strength to go through my various seasons and wait with the expectation that you will grant me the desires of my heart. Amen

Day 5

Be True to Yourself

Scripture Reading: *"I will praise thee; for I am fearfully and wonderfully made: marvellous are thy works; and that my soul knoweth right well."*
Psalm 139:14

With over seven billion people in the world, it is safe to say there will always be someone more intelligent or beautiful than you are. Everyone is responsible for knowing who they are based on what God says. On a daily basis, work on being the best version of yourself. Stand firm in who you are and do not be swayed by the opinions of others. Do not allow people to make you feel 'less than' or that something is wrong with you because of the high standards you choose to hold.

God made everyone unique; it is up to each individual to walk into what God has called them to be. If you compromise your values and standards for others or water down who you are, this will only lead to frustration and regret. There is a possibility people will still be unable to handle who you are - even if you choose to compromise your standards. Know that you will not be everyone's choice or 'cup of tea' and you must be ok with that. Also, as you begin to evolve - expect to outgrow some people and relationships. If you are struggling in this area, I encourage you to declare the word of God over your life on a daily basis as reinforcement. It will resonate in your spirit and will eventually build your faith.

Day 5 - Be True to Yourself Reflections

1. Have your ever lost who you were trying to please others? If so, are those people still in your life today?

_____

_____

_____

2. If someone were to ask you to explain who you are, what would your response be?

_____

_____

_____

_____

  2b. Is this response a reflection of who God says you are?

_____

_____

_____

3. Do you find yourself consumed with the opinions of others?

_____

_____

_____

4. What steps are you currently taking to improve yourself or pursue what God has called you to do?

_____

_____

_____

_____

Be True to Yourself Prayer

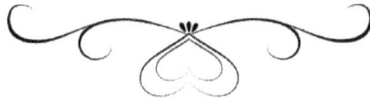

Lord, deafen my ear gates to the negative words spoken by others. I pray that I will have the faith to believe and walk into who your word says that I am.
Amen

Day 6

Where is Your Focus?

Scripture Reading: *"And the LORD answered me, and said, Write the vision, and make it plain upon tables, that he may run that readeth it"*.
Habakkuk 2:2

Even though God has the ultimate blueprint for your life, you should always have a vision. Anyone who does not have a life plan is operating like a ship without a compass. Can you imagine being on a ship that is sailing without a destination in sight? How do you think the passengers would feel? Life is similar to that scenario. Think about your gifts and talents to determine where you could potentially see yourself in the future and ask God to show you your life through His eyes. Once the vision is established - develop smaller, measurable goals and target dates. This will enable you to carry your vision. God will lead you to the provisions and divine connections to help you achieve your goals. This is why you have to make certain you can articulate your vision to others so they will know how to proceed. Be mindful to have those in your inner circle who are 'vision carriers' and not 'vision killers'. As you navigate through your vision, adjustments will need to occur based on the direction in which God is taking you. Be bold and soar like the eagle you are!

Day 6 ~ Where is Your Focus? Reflections

1. What is your vision for your life? Are you able to articulate it to others?

_____

_____

_____

_____

2. What areas are you gifted in? Are those gifts being used at the moment? Why or why not?

_____

_____

_____

_____

3. Have you consulted God to find how you can be used for His honor and glory?

_____

_____

_____

4. Did you discern whether those connected to you are a part of God's vision for your life?

_____

_____

_____

_____

_____

Where is Your Focus Prayer

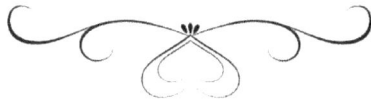

Father, give me the courage to step out on faith based on the God-inspired vision. Help me to recognize your provisions and divine connections - as they may not come the way I expect them to. Teach me to walk in your perfect timing so that the vision will come to pass in its correct season. Amen

Day 7

Where is Your Naomi?

Scripture Reading: *"Then Naomi her mother in law said unto her, My daughter, shall I not seek rest for thee, that it may be well with thee".* Ruth 3:1

Most successful people have someone who serves as a mentor that helps instruct them in different areas of life. It is vital that you find someone who is a forerunner to assist in your birthing process. Forerunners have the ability to walk you through unfamiliar territories and shift you as you come into who God has called you to be. Due to the seriousness of this relationship, be prayerful that God will direct and order your steps towards the right person. These people are not there to serve as your personal God or prophet; their purpose is to help guide you in the right direction. Remember, no matter how close you become with your mentor - refrain from allowing familiarity to get in the way. Always respect and give honor where it is due. As you progress, they will allow you to fly on your own and become less dependent on them. This process is similar to how God deals with 'babes in Christ' - giving only milk initially then progressing to 'meat' as a Christian grows in their faith.

Day 7–Where is your Naomi? Reflections

1. Do you have someone that can serve as a mentor in your life? If not, why?_____

_____

_____

_____

2. Have you identified the fruits or manifested evidence in your mentor's life?

_____

_____

_____

_____

3. Has your life improved or declined since having a mentor in your life?

_____

_____

_____

_____

4. Is your mentor causing you to be dependent on them? If yes, how? Do you think this is a healthy relationship?

_____

_____

_____

_____

_____

Where is your Naomi Prayer

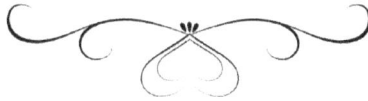

Father, bless me with a mentor who will lead me according to the will that You have predestined for my life. Give me the ability to recognize them when they come into my life and help me not to become too familiar with them. Amen

Day 8

It's a New Day

Scripture Reading: *"Behold, I will do a new thing; now it shall spring forth; shall ye not know it? I will even make a way in the wilderness, and rivers in the desert".*
Isaiah 43:19

Anytime God wishes to do something new in your life, a shift usually takes place. In some instances, the shift might be uncomfortable because He is now requiring you to move into an unfamiliar territory. A shift can range from the shedding of your inner circle, because some cannot go where God is taking you because of their mind-set, to requiring you to change location in order for you to accomplish the work that He has predestined you to do. As painful as the shift maybe, know that it is necessary and that it is all a part of God's plan. At times, you may feel timid - but exercise your faith and confidence in your Heavenly Father, knowing that His desire is not to harm you.

God may provide a glimpse into your future, but it is during the 'in-between' where many encounter difficulty. People must be encouraged and know that God will deliver them and set them free from every bondage they are experiencing. It makes no sense to pray, decree, and declare blessings in the atmosphere and not live in expectation that God will truly do a new thing in your life. Most people are not open to receive the blessing if it is not packaged the way they expect. It is crucial to renew your mind and ask God to reveal Himself to you in order to prevent you from missing Him in your due season.

Day 8 - It's a New Day Reflections

1. Are you able to discern what God is doing in your life now?

_____

_____

_____

_____

_____

2. Do you truly believe that God is doing a new thing in your life?

_____

_____

_____

_____

3. Do you believe that God has abundant blessings for everyone except for you? Why or why not?

_____

_____

_____

_____

4. What are some of the ways in which you can increase your faith level to believe what God says about you?

_____

_____

_____

_____

_____

It's a New Day Prayer

Father, I thank you for my new season. I ask that you give me the discernment to recognize what you are doing in my life so that I do not miss my appointed season. Amen

Day 9

Brokenness is Necessary

Scripture Reading: *"The sacrifices of God are a broken spirit; a broken and contrite heart, O God, you will not despise'.* Psalm 51:17

From the moment you accept Jesus as your personal Savior, the process of brokenness begins. You might ask, "How I can be sure of this?" Well as you go through life, you witness the world's system on how to approach situations and achieve desired results. You were taught that anything accomplished, was due to your strength or the strength of others. Because of this, God has to renew and retrain your mind how to navigate life using kingdom strategies and the leading of the Holy Spirit. Doing things God's way decreases your level of control, which causes a level of discomfort for many. It is during this process that God tears down the fruits of the flesh and any incorrect ideology; He then builds you back up with the fruits of the Spirit and a transformed mind. Despite this being a painful progression, I urge you to trust God; lean not to your own understanding and know that He desires nothing but His best for you.

1. Do you have the ability to praise God in your brokenness?

_____

_____

_____

2. Are you passing the tests that God is putting you through? If not, how long do you intend to deal with the same situation?

_____

_____

_____

_____

3. Do you feel you should be exempted from the process of brokenness because of your faithfulness? Why or why not?

_____

_____

_____

_____

4. Have you accepted the Kingdom way of life even though you may not understand it all?

_____

_____

_____

_____

_____

Brokenness is Necessary Prayer

Lord, purge me of all unrighteousness that would keep me from being in your presence. Help me to remain humble and committed to your process no matter how difficult it becomes. Amen.

Day 10

How Content are You?

Scripture Reading: *Not that I speak in respect of want: for I have learned, in whatsoever state I am, therewith to be content.*
Philippians 4:11

In today's society with social media running rampant, it is hard for people to be satisfied with their current state or possessions. Social media has become an illusion that fascinates many. Consequently, the focus has shifted to what people do not have and as a result - they are stressing themselves trying to keep up with others. This type of mind-set can lead to jealousy and covetousness, of which God warns us. Do you realize that individuals mainly post the good things they want you to see? How many people have you witnessed posting the unadulterated truth about themselves on social media? God knows your needs and He has promised to supply every one of them. Remember that God has not forgotten about you and He promises to give you the desire of your heart. In the meantime, learn how to be content in the state you are in until your change comes.

Day 10 - How Content are you? Reflections

1. Do you consider yourself to be an envious person?

_____

_____

_____

2. Do you feel substandard if you do not have what others have?

_____

_____

_____

_____

3. Are you trying to keep up with the latest hairstyles, fashion etc, because you feel the need to outdo others?

_____

_____

_____

_____

4. Are you as content in your real life as you appear to be on social media?

_____

_____

_____

_____

_____

How Content are You Prayer

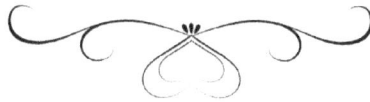

Lord, help me to stay in a state of gratitude with all that you have blessed me with. I look not to the left or to the right, but I look up to you. Give me the strength that will carry me through until my change comes.

Amen

Day 11

The Joys of Singleness

Scripture Reading: *There is difference also between a wife and a virgin. The unmarried woman careth for the things of the Lord, that she may be holy both in body and in spirit: but she that is married careth for the things of the world, how she may please her husband.* 1 Corinthians 7:34

Many singles view singleness as a form of punishment from God, but it is really a blessing. Singles are free to do whatever they choose and achieve goals that can potentially be more challenging to obtain when a mate is present. Truth is, I've had conversations with married women who admitted they wished they had maximized their time of singleness, because marriage is a lot of work and finding time to accomplish goals now is a bit more challenging.

Singles; do not worry, God knows your desire for marriage, but He must establish you first. He has to ensure that you are whole in order to prevent you from going into a marriage damaged or even with the wrong frame of mind. If you have never been married and desire to get it right the first time - or if you are divorced and desire to get it right the next time, then waiting on God is critical. Getting God's best usually require sacrifices and a waiting period. However, there is no need to fear because delayed does not equal denied. Are you establishing your life based on God's instructions while you wait or are you simply existing in life? Do you feel like you have to wait for your husband before you can attain certain goals? If this is your thought process, then you are not ready for marriage.

Marriage is not a fairy tale and if you cannot manage yourself, you will not be able to manage a home. Marriage is ministry and it represents God and His bridegroom (the church). Ladies, embrace your singleness and all God has in store for you during this season. Also, it is time to surrender your thoughts on marriage and singleness to God so He can give you His knowledge on what each entails and requires.

Day 11 - the Joys of Singleness Reflections

1. Do you date yourself by going to lunch etc. by yourself?

_____

_____

_____

_____

2. Are you living or simply existing in your single life?

_____

_____

_____

_____

3. Are you willing to be obedient to God and make the necessary sacrifices to wait on God's best for you?

_____

_____

_____

_____

4. Even though all marriages are different, have you taken anytime to speak with married couples to find out what makes a marriage successful? What are some of the things you learned?

_____

_____

_____

_____

_____

_____

The Joys of Singleness Prayer

God teach me how to live a successful single life until you send my God-ordained mate. Help me not to look at my singleness as a condition, but rather as a state that I can learn more about you and myself. Amen

Day 12

Heartbreak

Scripture: *"For his anger endureth but a moment; in his favour is life: weeping may endure for a night, but joy cometh in the morning"* Psalm 30:5

Experiencing heartbreak is never easy, as it signifies there is loss of a relationship. Despite the pain, we must thank God for keeping us from unseen dangers. There is a tendency to observe what is not there because you are so desperate for a relationship. This is why having trusted friends or family members are important, as it can aid with sound judgement. God allows us to see the warning signs and red flags, but people tend to drop their guard and discernment. Anytime this happens, be assured that trouble is on the horizon. Individuals begin tolerating behaviors from others that they ordinarily would not tolerate, thus disregarding all of their standards and values. Some even disregard friends and family members for the sake of a relationship.

Compromise is expected in relationships - but if you are the only one putting in effort, then it is time to move on. Singles - let go of what is not for you so that you may receive what God has for you.

Day 12 - Heartbreak Reflections

1. Are you still mourning the loss of your last breakup? How long has it been and are you really trying to get over that individual?

_____

_____

_____

_____

2. Why do you think you keep attracting the same type of men?

_____

_____

_____

_____

3. Have you ever compromised your values and standards for a relationship and still lost it?

_____

_____

_____

_____

4. Are you willing to give God your broken pieces so He can heal you? If no, what is preventing you from doing so?

_____

_____

_____

_____

Heartbreak Prayer

Father, mend my broken heart and fill it with your love. Help me to be cognizant to the red flags that you are showing me. Give me the courage to walk away from any impending danger. Amen.

Day 13

God's Temple

Scripture: *"What? Know ye not that your body is the temple of the Holy Ghost which is in you, which ye have of God, and ye are not your own?"*
1 Corinthians 16:9

As a representative of the Kingdom of God, we must adorn ourselves like someone who belong to a royal priesthood. Ladies, be mindful that simplicity and elegance is respected when beautifying yourselves. Our bodies are earthen vessels that God uses to accomplish His will here on earth. Because of this, God is holding us responsible for how we treat our bodies. We must be mindful that if we are not feeding our bodies with the proper nutrition, exercise and receiving sufficient rest - then it will be difficult to do what God requires. The Holy Spirit resides in us and is one of the ways in which God communicates with His children. We must remain cognizant of our conversations, thoughts and behavior and we must do everything possible to not defile our bodies by grieving the Holy Spirit. This means we must put away all of the fruits of the flesh such as anger and slander, that hinder the Holy Spirit from operating through us.

Day 13 - God's Temple Reflections

1. How well do you take care for your body? Do you think God would be pleased?

_____

_____

_____

2. How do you ensure that you do not grieve the Holy Spirit with your thoughts or conversations?

_____

_____

_____

_____

3. Is your behavior reflective of your Heavenly Father?

_____

_____

_____

_____

4. Do you use the book of Esther as an example of how to adorn your temple?

_____

_____

_____

_____

_____

_____

_____

_____

God's Temple Prayer

Lord, give me insight on how to properly care for your temple. Help me to be more aware of your Holy Spirit so I may please you in all that I do. Amen.

Day 14

Temptation

Scripture Reading: *"There hath no temptation taken you but such as is common to man: but God is faithful, who will not suffer you to be tempted above that ye are able; but will with the temptation also make a way to escape, that ye may be able to bear it"*
1 Corinthians 10:13

In life, there will be various trials and tests known to man. In reality, one of the biggest tests or temptations singles will always face is learning how to keep the flesh under subjection. With the number of people wanting to 'test drive the car' before purchasing the car - singles must know how to stand their ground by letting their 'no mean no'. When dating, singles must use wisdom to know when the way of escape is available to them. Abstaining from sexual activity is crucial to prevent grieving the Holy Spirit and creating unnecessary soul ties that will need to be broken. To grieve the Holy Spirit means to disappoint him and when this happens, He leaves our presence because He hates sin. If we are sincere in asking for forgiveness - it will be given. Nevertheless, we must not take for granted the grace and mercy extended towards us. Likewise, how would you feel professing Christianity and not conforming to what you are preaching? Do you think others would see you as credible if they discovered the truth? In some instances, we are the only 'Bible' non-believers will know. As a result, we must try daily not to contradict the word of God and confuse non-believers.

Day 14 – Temptation Reflections

1. Do you have anyone that you can speak to in confidence and discuss your emotions in the event you are thinking about making an irrational decision?

_____

_____

_____

2. Do you have a mentor that you can be accountable to especially if you are dating?

_____

_____

_____

3. How important is celibacy to you and are you practicing it? Why or why not?

_____

_____

_____

_____

_____

4. Are you hesitant about telling a guy that is interested in you that you are abstaining from sex? Why or why not?

_____

_____

_____

_____

_____

_____

Temptation Prayer

Lord, in my moment of weakness you are my strength. I ask that you provide me with a way of escape whenever it is needed. Help me to build up my spirit so that I may not fulfill the lust of the flesh.

Amen

Day 15

Loneliness

Scripture Reading: *"When my father and my mother forsake me, then the Lord will take me up"*.
Psalm 27:10

Feeling lonely is never a good feeling. There are instances when you can be in the presence of friends and family members and still feel alone. How many of you have experienced this scenario before? In that moment, you may feel lost and wonder how it is even possible. Do not allow loneliness to cause you to settle and be with someone that God has not ordained for you to be with as this will only compound the delicate situation that you are currently experiencing. It is during those times when you will need to set your face like flint before God and commune with Him to determine what He is saying concerning you.

The teacher (God) is usually silent when you are taking the test even though this is a difficult process. You must know and understand that even Jesus felt lonely as He hung on the cross - but He knew it was part of His assignment and that it was for a greater purpose - to save humanity. God promises that He will never leave or forsake you and this is a guarantee of which you can be sure.

Day 15 – Loneliness Reflections

1. Do you still feel the need for a physical presence even though you know God is there with you?

_____

_____

_____

_____

2. What do you do when you become lonely?

_____

_____

_____

_____

3. Is your expectancy that marriage will cure your feelings of loneliness?

_____

_____

_____

_____

4. Has loneliness driven you into the arms of someone that has hurt you before? If yes, did you feel any better while in their presence?

_____

_____

_____

_____

Loneliness Prayer

Lord, in my times of loneliness I look to you for comfort. I stand on your word that says that you will be with me even until the end of time. Amen

Day 16

Battlefield of the Mind

Scripture Reading: *"Casting down imaginations, and every high thing that exalteth itself against the knowledge of God, and bringing into captivity every thought to the obedience of Christ"*
2 Corinthians 10:5

From the beginning of time until now, there has been a constant struggle of the mind. In your time of singleness, the enemy will always have you focus on your current situation and not your final destination. Thoughts that run through your mind range from whether or not you are good enough - to whether or not God has forgotten you. It is during these times when you must reject the negative thoughts and replace them with the word of God concerning your life. If you are unsure of where the thoughts are coming from - always remember that God's word speaks life and the enemy's words bring defeat. Remember that the enemy will attack individuals at their lowest point. He will also attempt to cause a period of isolation from others. If this occurs, it will be beneficial to speak with someone who can assist you in this area.

Another exercise to assist with mind battles is to write what the word of God says about you and declare it daily.

Day 16 – Battlefield of the Mind Reflections

1. What are you thinking about daily? Do you know all actions are conceptualized before they are actually performed or carried out?

_____

_____

_____

_____

2. Who do you believe concerning your destiny, God or the enemy?

_____

_____

_____

_____

3. How often do you pray against mind battles?

_____

_____

_____

_____

4. Do you intentionally train your mind to think about the Word of God to combat the vain imaginations?

_____

_____

_____

_____

Battlefield of the Mind Prayer

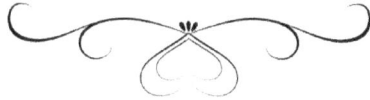

Lord, you promise to keep those in perfect peace whose minds are steadfast on you. Allow your Holy Spirit to bring me in remembrance of what your word says about me so that I can live successfully. Amen

Day 17

Heal Before You Deal

Scripture Reading: *"He sent his word, and healed them, and delivered them from their destructions".*
Psalm 107:20

After a breakup, it is important to take time to do some soul searching. When in relationships, people get used to relying on their mate to do things with and for them. Soul searching will help individuals find themselves as a single person who isn't tied to someone else. As you seek God, He will provide you with the necessary healing to fill all voids resulting from the breakup. He will teach you what perfect love is. It is normal to be single and you should avoid rushing into a relationship until the healing process is completed to prevent further damage to yourself or anyone else. Can you imagine meeting your God-ordained mate - but you are not completely healed? Do you think this relationship would last? Do you believe they would be able to measure up to all that you required if you did not perform any soul searching? There is no set time on how long this process should take. However, if you find yourself struggling in this area, you should seek help. You will be aware when it is time to enter the dating scene again.

Day 17 - Heal Before You Deal

Reflections

1. Do you feel you need to consult a professional to help you to heal, why or why not?

_____

_____

_____

2. Do you go around intentionally hurting others because someone else has hurt you?

_____

_____

_____

_____

3. How desperate are you for your healing?

_____

_____

_____

_____

4. Do you think that God would send your purpose partner if you are not whole?

_____

_____

_____

_____

_____

_____

Heal Before You Deal Prayer

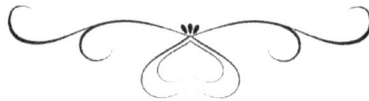

Lord, teach me what perfect love is so I may know how to love and be loved. I ask that you provide complete healing that will fill all the voids in my life.

Amen

Day 18

Your Boaz will Redeem You

Scripture Reading: "*Then Boaz said to the elders and all the people, "You are witnesses today that I have bought from the hand of Naomi all that belonged to Elimelech and all that belonged to Chilion and Mahlon. Moreover Ruth the Moabitess, the wife of Mahlon, have I purchased to be my wife, to raise up the name of the dead upon his inheritance that the name of the dead be not cut off from among his brethren, and from the gate of his place: ye are witnesses this day.*" Ruth 4:9-10

In the book of Ruth, you will find that Boaz proudly redeemed Ruth at the gates - which was a place of high esteem for all to see. This means that your Boaz will do the same for you. Singles; when a man is interested in you, he will pursue by going to the ends of the earth to be with you if he must. Finding excuses and playing games will not be a part of his character, as he will be a godly man. He will ensure that his affairs are in order before he takes you as his wife for all to see. If you are a single mother, know that he will accept the entire package that comes along with being with you. He will respect and honor you and will not ask you to comprise your values or standards just to accommodate his flesh or selfish ambitions. He will love and cherish you and desire nothing but the best for you. In spite of the weight of the wait, he will be worth the wait.

Day 18 – Your Boaz will Redeem You

Reflections

1. Do you have the ability to discern the pattern of men who are not serious about relationships or do you keep falling for the same type of guy?

_____

_____

_____

2. Do you have a list with the characteristics of what you want in a husband? Is your list reflective of the word of God?

_____

_____

_____

_____

3. Why do you feel you are still single?

_____

_____

_____

_____

4. Did you work on breaking all generational curses and soul ties that may hinder you from becoming a wife?

_____

_____

_____

_____

Your Boaz Will Redeem You Prayer

Father, I thank you for my Boaz and I ask that you help him locate me at the appointed time with ease. I pray that my spirit will be open and I will have the mind-set to receive him when you send him. Amen

Day 19

What Does God Say About Marriage?

Scripture Reading: *"And the rib, which the L**ORD** God had taken from man, made he a woman, and brought her unto the man. ²³ And Adam said, This **is** now bone of my bones, and flesh of my flesh: she shall be called ¹Woman, because she was taken out of Man. Therefore shall a man leave his father and his mother, and shall cleave unto his wife: and they shall be one flesh.'* Genesis 2:22-24

The institution of marriage should not be entered into causally. To stand before God and make a covenant to love and cherish another is very serious. Singles, you are indeed the missing rib to your God-ordained mate and he is looking for you. Be sure to make the best out of your single life because when you become married, you will be required to operate as one flesh with your mate. You will have to uproot your entire life and make adjustments as it relates to your new life with your husband. Make sure that you are prepared to meet the demands of your husband even when you do not feel like it. Be sure to discuss things that can become potential issues, such as finances and children. For those who are entering blended marriages, it is crucial that the children's emotional needs are met to prevent it from becoming a hindrance to the marriage.

Married couples must be certain to define their roles based on the word of God. You might ask how can this be done. Searching the scriptures is a good place to begin. The fact of the matter is that most people are so focused on the wedding - they forget to prepare for the actual marriage, which begins after the wedding reception. Reality now begins to set in; 'this is the person I decided to spend the rest of my life with'. How are your emotions now that the hype has died down and the actual work begins? Singles, do you think you will have the ability to discern when your husband is 'going through' even without him saying? How do you feel about submission and what is your current disposition on leadership? Ladies, I encourage you to ponder on whether or not you are truly ready before making this life time commitment.

Day 19 - What does God Say about Marriage

Reflections

1. Do you believe you have a true understanding of the institution of marriage?

_____

_____

_____

2. Are there married persons in your life who can provide transparency into what a marriage can be like?

_____

_____

_____

3. Are you prepared to give up your selfish ambitions to compromise for the rest of your entire life?

_____

_____

_____

_____

4. Do you understand the true meaning of submission?

_____

_____

_____

_____

_____

_____

What does God Say about Marriage

Prayer

Father, provide me with your wisdom on the institution of marriage. Teach me exactly what my role is as it relates to being the best possible wife that I can be. Amen

Day 20

To Whom Are You Connected?

Scripture Reading: *"Be ye not unequally yoked together with unbelievers: for what fellowship hath righteousness with unrighteousness? And what communion hath light with darkness?"*
2 Corinthians 6:14

The Bible warns strongly against being unequally-yoked. Now, you may feel as though God is trying to control your relationships - but He is not. After all, He has given you His free will to choose. If you are a believer, being in an unequally yoked relationship (friendship or with a mate) can be very dangerous to your destiny.

For the sake of this devotion, we will discuss relationships (with a mate). In most cases, there is a difference in beliefs. The believer operates upon the principles of the word of God and the unbeliever functions according to the world's system. Given that statement, can you see why there is a potential for confusion? If you have been called to greatness - then settling for any man will not do. As difficult as it maybe, you must understand that an unbeliever does not have the capacity to comprehend who you are in Christ. If he does not have direction for himself

- do you think he will possess the ability to lead and help carry you to your destiny? According to the Bible, the male is supposed to be the headship; if the roles are reversed, it will only lead to chaos. Ladies, I admonish you to wait on God to prevent experiencing unnecessary heartaches.

Day 20 - To Whom Are You Connected

Reflections

1. What are your thoughts on a Christian marrying an unbeliever? Do you think this is ok, why or why not?

_____

_____

_____

2. Are you willing to derail your destiny out of desperation even if God says that a particular relationship is not for you?

_____

_____

_____

3. Do you recognize when persons are speaking negativity concerning the possibility of you getting married? If so how do you handle the negative remarks and how does it make you feel?

_____

_____

_____

4. How many persons in your life are encouraging you to pursue an unequally yoked relationship? Do you feel they have your best interest at heart? Why or why not?

_____

_____

_____

_____

To Whom Are You Connected Prayer

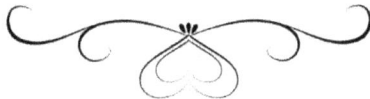

Father, help me to wait on you so that I may not derail your timing for my life. I ask that you sever all ungodly relationships hindering me from my next level. My prayer is that my connection will be to those who will assist in birthing forth the promises of God in my life. Amen

Tavara Johnson 86

Day 21

The Value of Your Story

Scripture Reading: *"And they overcame him by the blood of the Lamb, and by the word of their testimony; and they loved not their lives unto the death".*
Revelation 12:11

As we navigate through life, we will endure many trials and tribulations. Like many of you reading this devotional - the enemy will have you believe that you are the only one experiencing feelings of loneliness, rejection and curiosity about God's timing for your life. News Flash! All of us have been there - the only difference is that some choose to disclose their experiences and others do not for fear of what people may think or simply because they are trying to maintain a perfect image. You have the power to declare blessings and speak life over your circumstances. The more you share your testimony, through God's leading - you might be surprised to learn who you will inspire and who would provide you with support based on their testimony as well. No matter the intensity or depth of the experiences – remember, it would have been a challenge for all.

Day 21 – The Value of Your Story Reflections

1. Are you confident in your testimony and believe that others will obtain a level of freedom when you share it? Why or why not?

_____

_____

_____

_____

2. How transparent are you when sharing your testimony with others?

_____

_____

_____

_____

3. Do you feel you are relatable to others? Why or why not?

_____

_____

_____

_____

4. How does it make you feel to know that others encountered similar experiences as you did even though you felt like you were all alone?

_____

_____

_____

_____

The Value of Your Story Prayer

Lord, give me the wisdom to know to whom and where I should share my testimony. I ask that you bring those into my life who have the ability to encourage me through what they overcame and that I may do the same. Amen

Day 22

The Value of Prayer

Scripture Reading: *"Pray without ceasing."*
1 Thessalonians 5:17

The Bible advises us to remain in a prayerful posture. Being in a prayerful position involves having a heart of gratitude and always keeping the lines of communication open with God (it is not logical for a person to stay kneeling at a bedside continuously). Individuals must be mindful that prayer is simply talking to God. The length of your prayers does not affect how the hand of God moves - but rather the condition of your heart.

Anytime negative thoughts and doubt enter your mind, you can say a prayer to remove those thoughts. When we pray we are expressing to God that we are in need of Him and that we are unable to go through life on our own. Any time God shows you His goodness or manifested blessings, you should thank Him with a grateful heart. It is also during these times when you can pray for your potential mate, as you are not aware of the trials and tribulations he might encounter or is currently facing. In fact, I encourage you to develop a habit of praying for your mate so that when he comes - you would have already prepared for the new addition to your life.

Day 22 - The Value of Prayer Reflections

1. Do you know how to pray and did you ask the Holy Spirit to teach you?

_____

_____

_____

2. How often do you pray? Explain.

_____

_____

_____

_____

3. Do you incorporate fasting into your prayer life?

_____

_____

_____

_____

4. Do you only pray when you need something from God? How do you think this makes Him feel?

_____

_____

_____

_____

_____

_____

_____

_____

The Value of Prayer

Prayer

Father, help me to be in a prayerful state at all times. In times when I do not how to express myself, I ask that you intercede on my behalf. Amen

Day 23

Rejection for Redirection

Scripture Reading: *"And we know that all things work together for good to them that love God, to them who are the called according to [his] purpose".*
Romans 8:28

Rejection involves the denial of something. There are times when all opportunities seem closed off because you are constantly hearing the word 'no' and no matter how you attempt to create movement in your life, you encounter stagnation. Always remember that God not only open doors - He closes them as well. He allows this in order to redirect you towards your destination.

The human eye is limited in how far it can see and we must remember this. However, God has the ability to foresee situations and circumstances you are unable to discern. Anything that will bring calamity - He blocks for your protection. Often, people have a tendency to become angry with God for not allowing what they desire to manifest within their timing. Can you recall a time when you desired a relationship so badly and God said no? How did it make you feel? I am certain that the all-knowing God showed you months later *why* He said no. Now, how did you feel once He revealed the reason why the relationship did not come to fruition? Trust the blue print God has for your life, because He is constructing His masterpiece which is you!

Day 23 - Rejection for Redirection

Reflections

1. How well do you handle rejection?

_____

_____

_____

2. Do you believe there is purpose in your rejection?

_____

_____

_____

3. Do you believe the call of God on your life determines your level of rejection?

_____

_____

_____

_____

4. Do you believe that God is punishing you when you experience rejection? Why or why not?

_____

_____

_____

_____

Rejection for Redirection Prayer

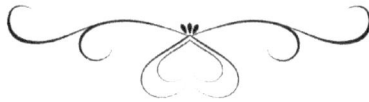

Abba, I thank you for redirection no matter how painful it may be. I trust you to lead and guide me every step of the way. Amen

Day 24

Secret Place

Scripture Reading: *"Thou art my hiding place and
my shield: I hope in thy word"*
Psalm 119:114

There are seasons in your life when God will decide to hide you in His secret place. It is during these times when you may experience what might be described as a 'dry place' or valley. In the valley is where God prunes and develops character and this process can be extremely painful. This scenario is similar to that of David's experience, when he was out in the field tending to sheep with no one in sight. You will experience instances where God will have you go unnoticed to others and you will feel alone. It is almost as if there is a 'do not enter sign' on a door preventing persons from entering. For many, the silence will become so real, you will have the ability to hear and feel it in your life. However, during this time - your relationship with God will begin to blossom even more and take on an entirely new meaning. You will have a special glow from being in the presence of God that individuals will notice, and they will wonder what is occurring in your life.

The secret place can be difficult if you have not discerned your location, have become weary and hope is lost. Know that God is not trying to harm you and your attitude concerning your dry season will determine how well you navigate it through.

Day 24 Secret Place Reflections

1. Do you know what season of your life you are in?

_____

_____

_____

_____

2. How often do you trust God to protect you at all times?

_____

_____

_____

_____

3. Do you know how to enter the secret place?

_____

_____

_____

_____

4. What have you learned from being in the secret place?

_____

_____

_____

_____

_____

Secret Place Prayer

Lord, I thank you for my secret place. Give me the grace to traverse through every dry season of my life. Help me to recognize the purpose of the secret place so that I do not become bitter. Amen

Day 25

Why Are You Fearful?

Scripture Reading: *"For God hath not given us the spirit of fear; but of power, and of love, and of a sound mind".*
2 Timothy 1:7

As believers, we are called to be bold and courageous. It is important to know that having the spirit of fear is not a characteristic of God. Some are fearful because of the hurt experienced by a former significant other or from the pressures of society. Individuals who are still recovering from past hurts must ensure that they work on ridding themselves of the spirit of fear to prevent sabotaging potential relationships. Witnessing peers achieve 'high esteem' status, causes an internal panic within many. As singles get older and their biological clocks tick - some are afraid they will never get married and believe the lies of the enemy spoken to them through others. It is imperative that you cancel all negative words spoken against you accomplishing marriage, because if you do not - you are unknowingly agreeing with the declarations released over you.

Ladies, it is better to be single, than to settle and endure undue stress because of a fear of being alone. My prayer is that you avoid making a decision you will regret that has the potential of having long-term repercussions. In most cases, fear is present due to the lack of trust in God. I admonish you to spend more time with God so that He can replace fear with faith. Lastly, do not cast your confidence away in God because at the right time, He will send your God-ordained mate.

1. Do you believe that you will get married? Why or Why not?

_____

_____

_____

2. When was the last time you cried because you are not married yet?

_____

_____

3. Do you believe that God is preparing you and your mate at the same time?

_____

_____

_____

4. Are you aware that your journey will be different from everyone else's? Why do you think God ordained it that way?

_____

_____

_____

_____

_____

_____

Why Are You Fearful Prayer

Lord, I cancel the spirit of fear from my life and I release any anxiety that I may have. I choose to trust your plans and your timing for my life. Amen

Day 26

Forgiveness

Scripture Reading: *If you forgive others the wrongs they have done to you, your Father in heaven will also forgive you. But if you do not forgive others, then your Father will not forgive the wrongs you have done.*
Matthew 6:14-15

One of the most difficult things in life is letting go of the past in order to move forward. Many are still holding onto situations that happened years ago, whether they were personally involved or it involved close family members. Since God does not hold us to our past and throws it in the sea of forgetfulness - I believe we should follow His example and do the same. Letting go involves making a conscientious decision to forgive someone.

The Bible advises us to forgive seventy times seven. Initially you will not feel like you have forgiven the person. Once you petition God for help in truly forgiving - He will assist you. Be mindful that this process can take a while depending on the nature of the offense. For example, a victim who suffered abuse at the hands of a significant other will probably take longer to forgive versus someone who had money stolen by a family member. As God begins to perform open-heart surgery on you, healing will take place. Healing can be gradual or instant, depending on how God chooses to move. You will know that forgiveness has truly occurred when you can be in the presence of the one who hurt you and ill feelings no longer remain. When this happens, give God thanks and praise.

Day 26 - Forgiveness Reflections

1. Make a list and think about all those that you need to forgive for the wrong they have done to you.

_____

_____

_____

_____

_____

2. Do you know that forgiveness is more of a benefit to you than the other person?

_____

_____

_____

_____

3. Do you feel that unforgiveness is hindering some of your prayers?

_____

_____

_____

_____

4. How often do you repent? Have you forgiven yourself for past mistakes?

_____

_____

_____

_____

_____

Forgiveness Prayer

Lord, help me to forgive those who have wronged me. Fill me with your love that I may experience the complete healing that you have for me. Amen

Day 27

Rehearsing the Past

Scripture Reading: *"Remember ye not the former things, neither consider the things of old"*
Isaiah 43:18-25

Because we are imperfect creatures, we have all made mistakes in our lives. Yes, there may be decisions in the past you may regret or there may be people who have hurt you - but you must let it go. If you continue to rehearse past hurts or mistakes, it will be difficult for you to move forward in life. The feeling of stagnation will only compound your feelings of guilt, increasing your frustration. How long do you intend to mourn in this manner? It is imperative to remember that life is all about progression and God's desire is for you to go from glory to glory.

Once you were repentant in seeking God's forgiveness, He has forgiven you and is no longer holding your past against you. After God has forgiven you, ensure that you not only forgive others - but forgive yourself as well. Instead of dwelling on the past - use past mistakes and hurts as fuel to take you to your next level. The Bible states that all things work together for your good. This means the good, bad, ugly - as well as mistakes. This is all a part of your testimony and journey. It is time to come from out of the ashes and embrace your future. Allow God to heal you and work on your heart so that you can be the woman He has called you to be. Remember only you can hold *you* back!

Day 27 - Rehearsing the Past Reflections

1. How does rehearsing the past add value to your life?

_____

_____

_____

2. Are you ready to release your broken pieces? Do you believe that no matter what broken pieces you may have, God can make them whole again?

_____

_____

_____

_____

_____

3. Do you have feelings of condemnation or joy after reliving your past? If there are feelings of condemnation, what does the Bible say about condemnation?

_____

_____

_____

_____

_____

4. Do you know that God allowed a saviour in the form of Jesus Christ to come so you can be freed from your past?

_____

_____

_____

_____

Rehearsing the Past Prayer

Father, help me to not dwell on the past so that I can walk in the fullness of all you have called me to be. My desire is to move forward so I can assist others who are struggling with rehearsing their past. Amen

Day 28

Virtuous Woman

Scripture Reading: *"Who can find a virtuous woman? For her price is far above rubies. The heart of her husband doth safely trust in her, so that he shall have no need of spoil"*. Proverbs 31:10-11

Everyone has their version of a virtuous woman - but is it according to the word of God? A virtuous woman is one who serves God and desires to follow His commandments. She respects her husband, provides a place of safety for him and he can trust her. He delights in her and trusts her to ensure that the affairs of the home are handled. It is important that singles work on becoming whole before getting married. Some areas where singles need to prepare include but are not limited to; knowing how to manage finances and their personal place of residence, as well as grooming. You must have the ability to add value to a man and be the helpmate God designed you to be. You must be willing to give of yourself unselfishly, even when you do not feel like it. A virtuous woman is one whom many admires. She has the ability to carry her husband and children in the spirit. In order to achieve this, a consecrated life is necessary. A foundation of prayer is also crucial for achieving success as a virtuous woman. As a virtuous woman who is in preparation mode - you should ensure that you are living life while you are waiting and working within God's calling. Choose to make a difference among those not only in your family, but in your community as well.

Virtuous Woman Reflections

1. What qualities do you possess that you feel make a virtuous woman?

_____

_____

_____

_____

_____

2. What steps have you taken to enhance your current abilities? Have you developed a vision or timeline in hopes of achieving this?

_____

_____

_____

_____

3. Do you consider yourself to be realistic or materialistic?

_____

_____

_____

4. How well do you have the ability to manage your own personal affairs? Do you feel like there is room for improvement?

_____

_____

_____

_____

_____

Virtuous Woman Prayer

Father, help me as I prepare to be the virtuous woman you have called me to be. I ask that you not let my feet slide as you guide me along the way. Show me how to be an example for all to see. Amen

Day 29

Guard your Heart

Scripture Reading: *Keep thy heart with all diligence; for out of it are the issues of life.*
Proverbs 4:23

We must be intentional about guarding our hearts, as the enemy will use a variety of weapons to attack it. The attacks usually originate from situations we are faced with that can sometimes lead to disappointment, discouragement, rejection or even disillusionment. It is during these times when you may become despondent and tempted to quit on God or in many areas of your life. As difficult as it may be, you must learn to trust that God is working out every situation on your behalf. Even with tears in your eyes, you have to be mindful of the words you speak because life and death is in the tongue. This is how you guard your heart. If you do not guard your heart, it can become bitter, angry or depressed - making it challenging for others to be around you. In addition - if you harden your heart towards God and what He is trying to accomplish in your life, your process or journey can become even longer. Allow the Lord to move on your heart and trust that He will not lead you astray. Be deliberate about protecting what comes into your spirit, as there are many things competing for your attention. If you lack wisdom - ask God for it and He will lead you. Lastly, remember to persevere in the face of difficulties - as you are more than a conqueror.

Day 29 - Guard your Heart Reflections

1. Are you someone who wears your feelings outwardly?

_____

_____

_____

2. Are you easily shaken by situations that may not occur as expected? If yes, what are some of the ways in which you can build your spiritual muscles?

_____

_____

_____

_____

_____

3. How has being taken advantage of cause you to react differently? Do you believe the changes you made are healthy and has not made you bitter?

_____

_____

_____

_____

_____

4. How often do you perform a heart check?

_____

_____

_____

_____

_____

Guard your Heart Prayer

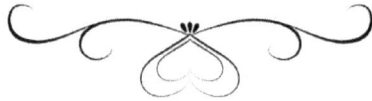

Lord, give me the wisdom to guard my heart. Help me not allow any of life's circumstances to get the better part of me, causing me to be despondent towards you.

Amen

Day 30

Be Still

Scripture Reading: *Be still, and know that I am God: I will be exalted among the heathen, I will be exalted in the earth.*
Psalm 46:10

For most people being still is an extremely difficult task, as they are accustomed to constantly being in overdrive. The continuous demands of life such as accomplishing goals and tasks, present an adrenaline rush like none other. For God to issue a command to be still indicates that some people are busy – but are achieving nothing. Many are working in their own strength and not acknowledging God. The Bible warns that there is a time for everything under the sun and this includes having peace and quiet times. As difficult as it might be, it must be an intentional decision to be still before God. If you are in need of help, ask your Heavenly Father for the strength to be still and spend time with Him so that you can bring your thoughts into focus concerning Him.

Focusing on God allows opportunities to increase your knowledge of who He is and your confidence in Him. Patterns and habits of being still and spending time with

God should be a lifestyle and second nature. Evaluate who God is to you and determine if He is truly the God of your life when everything else competes for your time and attention. Search your heart in hopes of concluding if there is evidence or fruit in your life that speaks to your identity in Christ. No matter what is happening around you, never neglect to spend quality time in the presence of God, as this is where healing, freedom and everything else you can think of happens. Know that God desires to show Himself strong on your behalf because He loves you.

Day 30 - Be Still Reflections

1. How often do you spend quiet time with God?

_____

_____

_____

2. Do you feel spending time with God makes a difference in how you handle various situations throughout your life? If yes, how?

_____

_____

_____

_____

3. Does your relationship with God only involve you giving Him a to-do list? If yes, how do you think He feels?

_____

_____

_____

_____

4. What are some ways in which you can show better appreciation and gratitude for God?

_____

_____

_____

_____

_____

_____

Be Still Prayer

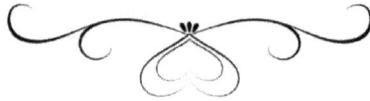

Lord, I thank you for your goodness and mercy even when I am undeserving of it. Help me to be still in your presence so that I will know the God of my salvation. Amen

Daily Declarations for Singles

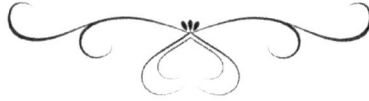

♥   I decree that the Lord strengthens me with all of His might according to His glorious power and because of this I receive patience and longsuffering. ~ Colossians 1:11

♥   I declare that every word that proceeds out of the mouth of God concerning my life will not return unto Him void, but it will accomplish everything that He said it would. ~ Isaiah 55:11

♥   I will not be anxious for anything, but instead I will submit everything to God by prayer and supplication. I will give thanks knowing that He will hear my petition and provide me with the peace that surpasses all human understanding that will guard my heart and mind. ~ Philippians 4:6-7

♥   Lord, I believe that I can do all things through you because you provide me with strength. ~ Philippians 4:13

♥   I decree and declare that the Lord has commanded the blessings upon me and my storehouses and everything that I put my hands to shall prosper. ~ Deuteronomy 28:8

♥   I confess that I am my Father's daughter because He is mine and I am always with Him. ~ Luke 15:31

♥   I will hearken to God's commandment so that I can boldly decree and declare that I am the head and not the tail and that I am above only, and not beneath. ~Deuteronomy 28:13

♥   Father, I believe in your word and declare that my status has changed. I am no longer called forsaken or desolate, but I shall be called married and you will delight in me. ~ Isaiah 62:4

♥   I will arise and shine for my light has come and the glory of the LORD is risen upon me. ~ Isaiah 60:1

♥   The Lord daily loads me with His benefits. ~ Psalm 68:19

♥   I am fearfully and wonderfully made and I praise the Lord for His workmanship. ~ Psalm 139:14

♥ Lord, your word tells me that you withhold no good thing from them that walk upright before you, so I thank you for my God ordained mate. ~Psalm 84:11

♥ I decree and declare that the joy of the Lord will always be my strength.~ Nehemiah 8:10

♥ Lord, your word says that it is not good for man to live alone so I thank you for my purpose partner whom you have ordained for me because you knew me and fashioned me from the foundation of the earth. ~ Genesis 2:18

♥ Lord, I believe that you know the plans you have for me and they are to bless me with a great future. ~ Jeremiah 29:11

♥ Lord, I confess that whoever my marriage partner is, I will submit myself to him as you have commanded and when he finds me, he shall obtain favour because he would have found himself a good thing. ~ Proverbs. 18:22

♥ Father, I know you desire the best for me and in the perfect timing, you will release the blessings that would make me rich and add no sorrow. ~ Proverbs 10:22

♥　　　Lord, deliver me from every trap and snare of the enemy and give me victory over every temptation that I may not sin against you or myself. ~ 1 Corinthians 6 18-20

♥　　　I trust the Lord to lead me and guide my footsteps so they would not slide. I will not lean to my own understanding but acknowledge God in all my ways to ensure that I make the right decisions based on his instructions.~ Proverbs 3:5-6

♥　　　I confess that if I ever become lonely, I will remind myself that the Lord will never leave me or forsake me and that He has sent a comforter into the world to be with me always. ~ Deuteronomy 31:6

About the Author

Tavara Johnson is a native from the quaint island of Grand Bahama in the Bahamas.

She is dedicated and passionate for the pursuit of purpose. One of her greatest achievements was the launch of Jewels & Gems; an organization that help women discover healing and their ultimate purpose. Tavara has hosted empowerment events for women via Jewels & Gems and is also a mentor for young girls.

She is currently pursuing her Doctorate degree in the Ministry in Christian Counseling and holds a Master's Degree in Business Administration and a Bachelor's Degree in Technical Management.

Tavara is a professional that has been working in the Human Resources industry for the past nine years. Tavara believes she has been called to greatness, and has a responsibility to encourage and empower women and girls to take the journey. Her life's mantra is ***"People make time for whatever they are interested in"***.

To contact Tavara you can e-mail her at: tavarajohnson@hotmail.com

www.ingramcontent.com/pod-product-compliance
Lightning Source LLC
Chambersburg PA
CBHW071816090426
42737CB00012B/2109